THE ADVENTURES OF

King Arthur

Retold by
Angela Wilkes
Adapted by Gill Harvey

Illustrated by
Peter Dennis

Reading Consultant: Alison Kelly
University of Surrey Roehampton

Contents

Chapter 1

The sword in the stone

One stormy night, Merlin, a wise
old wizard, left King Uther's
castle. Under his cloak, he carried
a baby... the king's only son.

3

King Uther had given the baby to Merlin to keep him safe from his enemies. He never saw his son again.

Years passed and King Uther died. All over England, knights began fighting over which of them should be king. No one knew about Uther's son.

But Merlin knew. "All the knights nearby must come to the Abbey in London," he announced.

When they arrived, a strange sight met their eyes. In front of the Abbey was a big, square stone with a sword sticking out of it.

Merlin read the words on the stone. "Whoever pulls this sword from the stone is the true-born King of England."

One by one, the knights went up to try their luck. But not one of them could move the sword, not even a little way.

"The king isn't anyone here," said a bishop. "We'll hold a jousting tournament to find him. Spread the word across the land, so that everyone knows."

Make sure you tell everyone, now!

As news of the tournament spread, the country's excitement grew. Hundreds of knights came to London with their families and friends, and set up tents.

Everyone wants to be king.

One of these knights was Sir Ector. He rode to London with his two sons, Kay and Arthur. Kay had just become a knight, but Arthur was still too young. He was only sixteen.

Sir Ector found an inn near the tournament where they could spend the night.

Early next morning, they set out. Kay was very excited. He was about to joust with other knights for the first time. But halfway there, he stopped in a panic.

"I've left my sword at the inn!" he cried.

"I'll fetch it!" offered Arthur, quickly turning and galloping off.

But the inn was shut. Everyone had gone to the tournament.

"Where will I find a sword?" Arthur wondered, as he rode past the Abbey. As he glanced into the churchyard, he saw a sword, stuck in a stone.

Hurriedly, Arthur pulled out the sword and went to find Kay.

Arthur raced up to Kay.

"Here you are!" he said, handing his brother the sword.

Kay stared at it. He knew right away where it had come from.

Oh!... Er, thanks, Arthur.

But he didn't tell Arthur. Instead, he snatched the sword and rushed to find their father.

"Father! Look!" he shouted. "I have the sword from the stone. I must be the King of England!"

But Sir Ector was not easily fooled. "Really, my son?" he said and took both boys back to the Abbey.

Arthur returned the sword to the stone. Sir Ector and Kay tried to pull it out again, but it wouldn't budge. Then it was Arthur's turn.

The sword slid out easily. At once, Sir Ector and Kay fell to their knees.

Arthur was puzzled. "Why are you kneeling?" he asked.

"Read the words on the stone, sire," said Sir Ector.

But, father...

I'm not your real father, Arthur.

"When you were a baby, Merlin brought you to me to save your life," he explained. "Now we must tell everyone that you are the king."

When all the knights gathered together, Arthur was still the only one who could pull the sword from the stone.

"Arthur is king!" cried the crowd and knelt down before him.

So Arthur was crowned king and he set up his court at a place called Camelot.

Chapter 2

The Lady of the Lake

Arthur ruled fairly and wisely, giving help to anyone who asked.

One day, a young man arrived at Camelot. He was very upset. "My master was murdered by another knight!" he cried.

Arthur listened carefully to the story. The murderer was a knight named Sir Pellinore, who had sworn to kill every knight passing through his forest.

"I shall fight Sir Pellinore myself," said Arthur and rode out the very next day.

On the way, he met Merlin. "You must turn back," the wizard told him. "Sir Pellinore is one of the strongest knights in the world."

"Turn back? Never!" declared Arthur. "I must save my people from this menace."

Merlin sighed. "If you insist," he said. "But I'm coming with you."

Suddenly, a knight appeared between the trees.

Stop! I am Sir Pellinore!

"Come any closer and I'll kill you!" cried the mighty knight.

"Just try it!" Arthur shouted in return. With a thunder of hooves, the two men rode at each other, gripping their lances.

They hit each other so hard that their lances broke. A servant brought two more and they charged again. This time, Arthur was knocked from his horse.

Arthur clambered to his feet. "Come on!" he cried.

Are you brave enough to fight me with a sword?

Sir Pellinore jumped from his horse. The two men fought furiously. Then Sir Pellinore struck Arthur's sword with a massive blow and it broke in two.

"Ha! I've got you now!" shouted Sir Pellinore. "Surrender or die!"

Instead, Arthur hurled himself at the knight and wrestled him to the ground.

I don't give up that easily!

But Sir Pellinore was stronger than Arthur and soon had pinned him down.

"No mercy this time!" he growled and raised his sword to chop off Arthur's head. Then he heard a voice. It was Merlin.

Sir Pellinore, stop! You can't kill the king!

"Oh, yes I can!" declared Sir Pellinore. "If he lives, he'll never forgive me!"

As Pellinore spoke, Merlin cast a spell on the knight. Sir Pellinore slumped to the ground, snoring.

Sleep, brave knight and end your fight.

"He was brave, but dangerous," Merlin said to Arthur. "Asleep, he can't hurt anyone."

Merlin took the wounded king
to a hermit who lived nearby. The
hermit tended Arthur's wounds and
in a few days he was better.

But Arthur was worried. "Where
am I going to get a new sword?" he
asked Merlin.

Don't worry.
We'll go to the Lake
of Avalon.

Merlin's plan meant a long journey. After many days, they reached the Lake of Avalon, where a strange sight rose before them.

"A hand… holding a sword," whispered Arthur. "But who is the beautiful lady on the water?"

"The Lady of the Lake," Merlin replied.

The lady walked across the water to Arthur and offered her hand.

"My Lady," he said, bowing low. "I am here to ask for the sword."

"You may fetch it yourself," she said, with a smile.

The sword's name is Excalibur.

The lady showed Arthur a little boat, hidden in the reeds. He stepped in and the boat glided to the hand.

Arthur reached out for the sword in its beautiful scabbard.

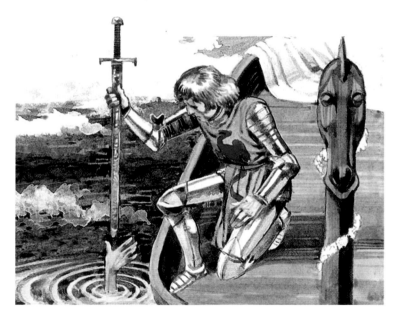

As he grasped it, the hand let go. Silently, it slid beneath the water and was gone.

When Arthur got back to shore, the lady had vanished. He showed Merlin the sword.

"It's wonderful!" Arthur exclaimed.

"It is," said Merlin. "But the scabbard is worth more. As long as you wear it, you will not bleed... however badly you are injured."

Arthur returned to Camelot and settled down to rule once more.

Chapter 3

The Round Table

A few years later, Arthur fell in love, with the beautiful Lady Guinevere.

"I want to marry her," he told Merlin. The wizard didn't think that was a good idea at all.

"You won't be happy," he warned.

But Arthur ignored Merlin's advice. "I love her!" he insisted.

Merlin sighed. "Well, it's up to you," he said. "I'll ask her father for you."

The king wishes to marry your daughter.

Sir Leo, Guinevere's father, was delighted. He was so pleased that he gave Arthur an enormous round table as a wedding present.

At Easter, Guinevere arrived at
Camelot. Hundreds of people came
to the wedding to see Guinevere
crowned queen.

I shall rule
happily with her
beside me.

Then Arthur led his bride into a
great hall, where a feast was
spread out on the round table.

The couple sat at the table
with Arthur's knights around
them. When everyone was settled,
Arthur stood to make a speech.

From now on,
you shall be known
as the Knights of the
Round Table!

"You must all swear to be noble and brave, and to help the weak and helpless. We shall meet here once a year to tell each other our adventures."

One by one, the knights stood up and swore to follow Arthur's rules. Arthur looked forward to a long and happy reign.

Chapter 4

Morgan le Fay

But all was not well in Camelot.
Arthur had an evil sister, Morgan
le Fay. She hated both Arthur and
her husband and loved one of
Arthur's knights, Sir Accolon.

Morgan was full of wicked plots.
Most of all, she wanted to be queen,
with Accolon as king. So she laid a
trap for Arthur.

One day, Arthur and Accolon
went hunting together and came
across a boat on a shimmering lake.

Look at that
amazing boat!

Beautiful maidens invited them
on board to eat and rest.

The maidens had prepared a
delicious feast.
Arthur and
Accolon ate,
drank and fell
asleep. Morgan's
spell was
working.

When Arthur woke up, he was
chained in a dark, dank prison.

"We've been
captured by a
knight named
Sir Damas,"
said another
prisoner.

Before long, a maid came to the prison. "Sir Damas will set you free, if one of you fights an enemy for him," she said.

"I'll do it!" cried Arthur, following the girl from the prison.

"Here is Excalibur," she said, handing him a sword.

Your sister Morgan sent your sword for you.

Meanwhile, Sir Accolon awoke in a different place, to find a dwarf standing in front of him.

"Morgan le Fay sent me," said the dwarf. "She begs you to fight an unknown knight."

She sent this sword for you.

"Of course!" said Accolon, who was a very noble knight.

Arthur and Accolon had fallen into Morgan's trap. She had set them up to fight each other. Hidden behind helmets, they didn't know who they were fighting.

Arthur attacked fiercely, but he was wounded many times. At last, with a mighty blow, Accolon broke Arthur's sword in two.

Accolon raised his sword...

Just as Arthur thought his life was over, the Lady of the Lake appeared. Raising her arm, she cast a spell on Accolon.

Drop the sword, foolish knight. Morgan has tricked you.

Arthur looked at the sword Accolon had dropped. "Excalibur!" he shouted and grabbed it.

With one sweep of Excalibur, Arthur knocked Accolon off his feet. As he fell, blood poured from a wound to his head.

"Kill me, noble knight," cried Accolon. "You have won."

Arthur heard his friend's voice in disbelief.

That sounds like... It can't be!

"Who are you?" demanded
Arthur, raising his visor.

"Accolon," whispered the other
knight, weeping as he saw Arthur.
"Morgan sent me," he croaked. "I
didn't know it was you…"

Quietly, Accolon lay back and died. Arthur was furious.

"Morgan will pay for this trick!" he promised and sent Accolon's body to his evil sister.

She was broken-hearted... but still determined to get the better of Arthur.

"I'll steal Excalibur!" she decided.

While Arthur lay recovering from his wounds, Morgan secretly visited him. She crept into his room as he slept, looking for his sword.

"I don't believe it !" she said to herself. Arthur was holding the sword in his sleep. But the magic scabbard was just lying there...

When Arthur woke up, he found the scabbard had gone. He called to the nuns who were taking care of him.

"Your sister Morgan visited you," they told him.

"Saddle my horse!" he cried. "I'm going after her!"

Morgan heard Arthur galloping after her and threw the scabbard into a lake. Then she cunningly turned herself and her servant into a rock.

Arthur hunted everywhere, but Morgan had completely disappeared. He had to give up.

Angrily, he banned her from Camelot forever.

Chapter 5

Sir Lancelot

One of Arthur's bravest men was a
knight named Sir Lancelot. He was
handsome and loyal and Arthur
trusted him. But there was a
problem. Over the years, Lancelot
fell in love with Queen Guinevere.

Arthur's enemies knew that Sir Lancelot loved Guinevere and decided to stir up trouble. Their leader was Arthur's nephew, Mordred. He planned to destroy Arthur and become king himself.

Lancelot loved talking to the Queen but he knew that Mordred wanted to make Arthur jealous. He thought if he met Guinevere in secret, they would be safe.

But Mordred's men were spying on them.

Mordred went straight to Arthur.
"Lancelot and Guinevere are traitors!" he said. Arthur didn't believe him.

That night, as Lancelot visited the Queen, Mordred and his men burst in on them. Grabbing his sword, Lancelot fought his way out and escaped.

"I have given you proof of their betrayal," Mordred told Arthur. "You know our custom. You must fight Lancelot, and Guinevere must be burned at the stake!"

Sadly, Arthur agreed.

On the morning the Queen was meant to die, Lancelot charged to the rescue. He cut her free and carried her away on his horse.

Arthur was secretly happy that Guinevere was safe, but he still had to fight Lancelot. Fierce battles followed. Finally, Lancelot fled to France. Arthur followed.

He left his nephew, Mordred, in charge. It was a big mistake. In no time at all, Mordred declared to England that Arthur had been killed and he, Mordred, was king.

The moment Arthur heard that Mordred had stolen his crown, he rushed back to England to fight his nephew. Mordred retreated, but many of Arthur's knights died.

I fear the fighting is over for me, sire.

Hush, now. Rest.

Arthur wept for his brave, dead knights, but he knew that Mordred was still a threat.

Chapter 6

The last battle

Arthur hunted Mordred down. Their final battle was so terrible that only four men were left alive: Arthur, two of his knights, and Mordred. Seeing Mordred, Arthur rushed at him with his spear.

As Mordred fell, he gave Arthur a huge blow to the head.

Arthur's knights saw their king struck and ran to him. Gently, they carried him to a little chapel near a lake... a lake Arthur recognized.

Arthur realized he was about
to die and handed his sword to Sir
Bedivere, one of the knights.

"Take Excalibur and throw it in
the lake," he told him. "Then come
back and tell me what you've seen."

I will do as you
say, my lord.

"This sword is beautiful!" Sir Bedivere thought. "It would be crazy to throw it away."

So he hid it among some reeds and went back to Arthur.

"What did you see?" Arthur asked him.

Sir Bedivere shrugged. "Nothing sire," he muttered.

"Then you didn't do as I said. Go back," Arthur told the knight.

So Sir Bedivere returned to the lake. As he hurled Excalibur into the water, a hand rose up and caught it, then sank again.

Bedivere rushed to tell Arthur. "Now help me to the lake before I die," the king instructed him.

As they reached the shore, a barge appeared. It carried the Lady of the Lake and three of her maids. Sadly, his two knights lifted Arthur into the barge.

"I am going to the Vale of Avalon to be healed," murmured Arthur. "Goodbye."

Silently, the barge floated away... and Arthur was never seen again.

Try these other books in the series:

The Amazing Adventures of Ulysses:
Ulysses sets out to rescue a Greek princess
and ends up in a ten-year war. But when he
tries to get home, his problems really start.

The Fairground Ghost: When Jake goes
to the fair he wants a really scary ride.
But, first, he must teach the fairground
ghost a trick or two.

The Incredible Present: Lily gets
everything she's ever wished for... but
things don't turn out as she expects.

Gulliver's Travels: Gulliver sets sail
for adventure and finds a country
beyond his wildest dreams...

Treasure Island: Climb aboard the
Hispaniola! Cabin boy Jim Hawkins is about
to set off in search of treasure. But there's
mutiny ahead. Jim must outwit cunning
pirate Long John Silver if he's to stay alive.

Series editor: Lesley Sims

Designed by
Katarina Dragoslavić

This edition first published in 2006 by Usborne Publishing Ltd.,
Usborne House, 83-85 Saffron Hill, London EC1N 8RT, England.
www.usborne.com
Copyright © 2006, 2003, 1981, Usborne Publishing Ltd.

64